Original title:
In the Quiet of Nature's Embrace

Copyright © 2025 Creative Arts Management OÜ
All rights reserved.

Author: Harris Montgomery
ISBN HARDBACK: 978-3-69081-224-5
ISBN PAPERBACK: 978-3-69081-720-2

The Soul's Retreat in Green

Under leaves, a squirrel prances,
Chasing shadows, taking chances.
A butterfly with too much fluff,
Sits on a flower, calling it 'tough.'

With every breeze, the grasses giggle,
As ants parade, they all wiggle.
A frog croaks jokes from his bog,
While bees bust moves; it's a dance of a fog.

Sunlight on the Thicket's Edge

Sunshine laughing on a branch,
A rabbit hops, thinks he can dance.
Caterpillars strut in style,
While the trees sway and smile.

A songbird sings with a silly tune,
Trying to impress a passing moon.
The grasshoppers chatter, plot a play,
While the worms just wiggle all day.

Timeless Tranquility in the Grove

A snail in a race, oh what a sight,
Taking his time, without a fright.
A nearby tree shakes off its bark,
Whispers to bushes, 'Let's make a park!'

The sun peeks in, a cheeky light,
While crickets crack wise in delight.
A fox with glasses reads a sign,
Declares all trees are simply divine.

Reveries on a Quiet Hilltop

From the top, a view so grand,
A goofball goat takes a stand.
He claims he's king of all he sees,
But sneezes loudly, ruffling leaves.

Clouds roll by, oh what a show,
A bluebird giggles, 'Where'd they go?'
On this hill, all worries cease,
Nature's humor gives us peace.

Serenity Found in the Stillness

Birds tweet gossip, oh what a scene,
Squirrels debate, who's the king of the green.
Each rustling leaf has a tale to tell,
Even the crickets are casting a spell.

Mice stretch in yoga, trying to find peace,
While butterflies flutter, as if they'd cease.
A laugh in the brook, it's funny as can be,
Nature's a jester, wild and free!

Beneath the Arch of Ancient Trees

Trees wear their wisdom like hats made of moss,
Their branches all dance, like they're the boss.
A raccoon takes selfies, it's quite the show,
While owls roll their eyes, 'Hey, don't be a foe!'

Beneath the green giants, every moment's a gem,
Bugs tap-dance on leaves, a true little phlegm.
Who knew that the forests had such a flair?
Humor's alive, spread it everywhere!

Murmurs of the Meadow at Dusk

Folks think it's peaceful when the sun goes down,
But rabbits are plotting, wearing their crown.
A family of deer joins for a dance,
They've mastered the tango, just look at that prance!

Fireflies flicker, like stars on the grass,
The frogs chirp loudly, 'come join us, alas!'
The grasshoppers giggle, they've brought their best puns,
In this funny meadow, everyone runs!

A Symphony of Shadows and Light

Sunlight winks at the frolicking fawn,
While shadows giggle, 'Let's play till the dawn!'
A chorus of crickets starts their grand song,
They laugh at the night, 'Oh, where do we belong?'

The moon rolls its eyes, 'Come on, take a break!'
As raccoons steal snacks, for goodness' sake!
Stars join the fun with a twinkling jest,
In a world filled with laughter, we're truly blessed!

A Tapestry of Blossoms

Bees wear tiny suits with flair,
Dancing 'round without a care.
Tulips giggle, petals sway,
Blooms tell jokes in bright array.

Butterflies play peek-a-boo,
Wings of color, always new.
"Why did the flower cross the lane?"
To find the bee that went insane!

Sounds of Solitude in the Glade

Squirrels chatter, plotting schemes,
While rabbits nap in sunny beams.
A chipmunk wins in hide-and-seek,
Laughing lots, now that's unique.

The trees gossip in rustling tones,
Sharing secrets without bones.
"Why did the crow sit on the wire?"
To know the scoop, as they conspire!

The Dance of Light Through Canopy

Sunbeams shimmy, all aglow,
Casting shadows; what a show!
"Do you think we should take five?"
Said the light, feeling quite alive.

Leaves twirl like they're at a ball,
"Who's the fairest of us all?"
Lights laugh, "We're all a bit chummy,
Especially when the breeze is funny!"

Beneath the Canopy of Whispers

Frogs croak their serenade so bold,
While toads share gossip, never old.
"Why did the lily pad break out?"
To join the fun without a doubt!

Crickets chirp their nightly tunes,
Practicing for their big cartoons.
"Where's the best spot to show my spark?"
"Just anywhere, just make your mark!"

Paths Worn by Wandering Thoughts

Wandering paths with my lopsided shoes,
The trees giggle softly, sharing my views.
A squirrel mocks me, with acorn in hand,
While I trip over roots, looking quite grand.

Thoughts like butterflies, flit in my mind,
Chasing them down, it's one of a kind.
They flutter away with each silly dance,
Leaving me chuckling, I'll take my chance.

Breath of the Earth in Stillness

The grass holds its breath, a secret it keeps,
While bugs play symphonies, as nature sleeps.
A breeze whispers by with a playful tease,
Scaring the crows, who squawk with unease.

Dandelions puff like fluffy white cakes,
While I flip and roll, making silly mistakes.
The earth's quiet laughter surrounds every turn,
As I leap into puddles, for joy I yearn.

Enfolded by the Arms of Twilight

The sun dips low with a wink and a grin,
As fireflies dot the sky, we both spin.
Even the moon in its silver attire,
Can't help but chuckle at this evening choir.

The crickets chatter, they've started their play,
Telling tales of the bugs who danced all day.
With my shadow stretching, I've become quite tall,
In this dusk of laughter, I'm having a ball.

Rooted in Rhythm: A Dance of the Divine

The trees tap their feet to the beat of the breeze,
While I join in the twirl, swaying my knees.
A rabbit joins in, with moves so absurd,
That I laugh 'til I cry at the sight of this bird.

Flowers sway gently, as if they could groove,
While I bust a move, trying to prove.
The chemicals spark, joy's rhythm I cheer,
In this dance with the wild, nothing's unclear.

Warmth of the Setting Sun

A turtle basks on a rock, oh what a sight,
With shades on its eyes, it feels just right.
A bird sings off-key, ever so bold,
As the sun drops low, the sky turns gold.

A squirrel pops popcorn, its favorite treat,
While ants hold a party, oh what a feat!
A mild breeze whispers, 'keep it light,
Even the daisies are laughing tonight.'

The Bowing Grasses of Humble Corners

The grass in the meadow sways and shakes,
As if it's dancing, making mistakes.
A rabbit hops in, doing a jig,
While a snail moves slowly, like a plump big.

The daisies gossip, 'What a wild scene!
That squirrel's got moves; he's fit and keen!'
The crickets begin to serenade,
As the sunset lights up their parade.

Nature's Embrace of the Unseen

A shy little shadow sneaks past a tree,
It's a raccoon, peeking, oh so carefree.
He stumbles on branches, trips on a root,
And blames it on squirrels—always a hoot.

The wind tickles petals, they giggle and sway,
While frogs hold a concert, croaking all day.
The sun winks down, as fireflies wink,
A summer night's laughter, more fun than you think.

Flourish of Serenity

Butterflies flutter in a crazy chase,
They bump into flowers, then giggle, 'Excuse us, grace!'
A wise old owl hoots, but what does he see?
Just chaos and jests in nature's decree.

Up high in the trees, a squirrel plays king,
With a crown made of acorns, he loves that thing!
The sun waves goodbye, as the stars come to glow,
And nature, it seems, puts on quite the show.

Reverberations of Dusk

As shadows dance with glee at dusk,
A raccoon juggles snacks, quite the husk.
Crickets giggle in the cool, soft air,
While owls debate who's the best at stare.

The sunset winks and blushes bright,
A squirrel slips, taking off in flight.
Leaves applaud with a rustling cheer,
As frogs croak jokes that only they hear.

The Tranquil Hour of Daybreak

At dawn, the world yawns, stretching wide,
A turkey struts with unearned pride.
The sun pokes fun, slips on its hat,
While cats play chase with a dancing rat.

Birds tweet gossip from high above,
About the owl who fell in love.
Soft breezes laugh, tickling the grass,
While morning glories bloom with sass.

Delicate Footsteps on Earth's Canvas

Tiny ants form a parade, so grand,
Carrying crumbs across the land.
A butterfly flutters, debating the path,
While a rabbit wonders who'll do the math.

Each footprint whispers a silly tale,
Of mischievous raccoons who stole the mail.
Flowers giggle as bees zoom near,
Painting the air with a buzz of cheer.

Songs of the Unbroken Silence

Beneath the stars, the crickets play,
While flatulent frogs hold a cabaret.
A raccoon serenades the moonlit night,
As fireflies flash in a disco light.

The trees sway, keeping time with the tune,
While owls hoot, 'Hey, we're up too soon!'
Even the rocks seem to chuckle and chime,
In nature's concert, everything's just fine.

The Calm After the Storm

Raindrops bounce on the lily pads,
While frogs in tuxedos glance and nod.
A squirrel's soaked, but still he's glad,
He shakes off water, looking like a god.

The clouds now part, the sun peeks through,
The worms throw parties, in mud they slide.
Ducks wear shades, a fashionable crew,
While trees stand tall, with branches wide.

Embraced by the Green Canopy

The branches wave like old friends do,
As I tiptoe past with a wink and a smile.
A chipmunk in a hat gives a sweet adieu,
While moss on the ground thinks it's all worth the while.

Beneath in the shade, ants march in line,
Debating grand plans for a picnic feast.
They bring acorns, berries… oh what a dine!
While a snail in a shell plays the role of the priest.

Still Waters Reflecting Solitude

The pond's a mirror, but oh what a tease,
It shows my reflection, a wild hair scare!
A fish jumps up, making waves in the breeze,
As turtles poke heads, pretending not to care.

A frog croaks loudly, claiming it's King,
While the dragonflies giggle, dancing on air.
A turtle rolls over, it's quite the act— bling!
As I chuckle softly, without a single care.

The Language of Leaves at Twilight

The leaves whisper secrets as they twirl and spin,
A gossiping breeze joins in for the fun.
They talk of the squirrels, and where they have been,
While crickets plan dances, 'til day is done.

A moonbeam peeks, with a laughter so light,
Illuminating shadows that prance and sway.
The fireflies flicker, just like stars at night,
As nature throws parties, in her special way.

Surrendering to the Song of Silence

Amid the trees, a squirrel prances,
Chasing clouds with comical glances.
A bird, in tune, sings off-key,
Making even the wise owl flee.

Butterflies dance in a fluttering beat,
One lands on a frog, who jumps in retreat.
The wind whispers jokes that make no sense,
While crickets chuckle in their defense.

The Still Heart of a Dappled Glade

In a sunbeam, a rabbit hops with flair,
Pretending to be crowned, a prince unaware.
The daisies giggle, their heads held high,
As the grass tickles toes passing by.

A turtle boasts of his speedy race,
While a snail rolls by, cool as space.
Laughter rings 'round in this leafy show,
As the leaves whisper secrets they want to bestow.

Whispers of the Woodland

A raccoon wearing a hat made of leaves,
Stand-up routine, oh how it weaves!
The trees applaud with rustling cheer,
As the fox jokes, 'Dinner's near!'

Beneath the branches, mystery lurks,
While the mushrooms giggle, doing their quirks.
Mice throw a party, they really know how,
Only to hide when a cat says, 'Wow!'

Serenity Beneath the Stars

Beneath the stars, a dance of delight,
A firefly disco, shining so bright.
The moon rolls her eyes at the glowing show,
While the owls soar high, all fancy and slow.

A raccoon winks, joining the groove,
As crickets croon, making their move.
Beetles are breakdancing, quite the surprise,
And the night laughs along, under starlit skies.

A Still Heart Amidst Blooming Fields

Butterflies flit by in a daze,
On flowers that laugh at the sun's warm rays.
A bumblebee buzzes with hopes of a snack,
While daisies giggle, saying, 'No, go back!'

The grass tickles toes like a playful friend,
As squirrels conspire, plotting to offend.
A ladybug skates on the petals so bright,
Saying, 'Life's a party, come join me tonight!'

The Call of Distant Peaks

Mountains beckon, 'Come up for a climb,'
But my legs are like jelly, oh dear, what a crime!
Chasing the view at a snail's gentle pace,
While the rocks look down with a stoic face.

The air grows thin, and my breath's in a knot,
Did I bring enough snacks? I really forgot!
At the summit, the scenery's quite grand,
But so is the call of the chili I planned!

The Rustle of Forgotten Dreams

Among the trees where the shadows play,
A chipmunk is pondering his afternoon fray.
He dreams of a life as a gallant knight,
But ends up just nibbling till the moonlight.

Leaves rustle as if they're sharing a tease,
'You think you're a hero? Just look at the breeze!'
Yet his tiny adventures are still full of glee,
In the grand world of nature, he's pretty carefree!

Moonlit Reverie in the Wild

The moon casts shadows where critters convene,
A fox in a top hat, so suave and so keen.
He tips it to owls who roll their wise eyes,
As fireflies dance under velvet night skies.

A raccoon jogs past, carrying change,
'For a midnight snack, I'll just rearrange!'
And all of nature breaks into a cheer,
As the night grows goofy, full of delight and cheer!

Pathways of Peace in the Forest

Squirrel in a hurry, chasing his tail,
Tripped over a root, oh what a trail!
Birds trading gossip, a feathered exchange,
All while the trees stand, calm and strange.

A rabbit hops by, looking quite grand,
With a monocle on, oh isn't it planned?
He gives a salute, with a twitch of his nose,
While the trees chuckle softly, in leaf-laden clothes.

The mushrooms are giggling, their caps in a twirl,
As frogs start a band, give jumps a whirl.
A deer in the distance, striking a pose,
Unaware he's a joke in this nature prose.

As dusk falls, the stars come to play,
Raccoons in tuxedos, all geared up for ballet.
Woodland shenanigans, laughter that stays,
In these pathways of peace, the forest displays.

Reflections Over Still Waters

The pond holds secrets, in ripples and sways,
Frogs croak their plans for hilarious plays.
A turtle in shades, on his shell he does lay,
Giving the fish life advice, come what may.

The ducks waddle over with perfect finesse,
Arguing who's got the best swimming dress.
They splash with laughter, oh such a delight,
Making the moon giggle all through the night.

A heron stands tall, casting shadows that dance,
Watching the minnows take part in a chance.
With a wink of an eye, he considers his hunt,
While dragonflies tease him, oh how they taunt!

The reflections shimmer, bringing joy to the night,
As fireflies twinkle, their lanterns so bright.
Nature's comedians, in a watery show,
In the stillness, their humor begins to flow.

The Silent Watcher of the Meadow

A butterfly flutters, a comedian in flight,
Tickling the daisies, taking delight.
A grasshopper laughs, he's got jokes to impart,
Turning a simple leap into fine art.

The owl in the tree tries not to snore,
But the sheep down below just want to explore.
They trample the clovers, making a mess,
While the owl rolls his eyes, in feathery stress.

A cricket strikes up a tune, oh so loud,
Bringing the ants together, a tiny crowd.
They form a conga line, with little feet bound,
Unaware of the watcher that looks all around.

As twilight blankets the meadow so grand,
The stars join the jig, giving twinkles on hand.
A party of nature with laughable cheer,
With the silent watcher enjoying it near.

Nature's Gentle Lullaby

In the arms of the forest, where laughter runs free,
A bear wears pajamas, all fluffy, you see.
He snores like a thunderstorm, louder than rain,
While nearby the bunnies find it all quite insane.

The wind plays a tune with the rustling leaves,
Scoffing at rabbits hiding behind their sleeves.
While hedgehogs giggle, all rolled up in fright,
What's scarier than bear pajamas at night?

The nightingale sings her sweet, silly song,
Enticing the owls to join in along.
They hoot out of rhythm, a not-so-melodious crew,
While the fox takes a bow, how do you do?

The stars twinkle softly, like lights on a stage,
As nature performs, turning up the page.
In this lullaby woven with fun and delight,
Every creature joins in for a wonderful night.

Caress of Daybreak on Sleeping Fields

Morning light tickles the grass,
Waking flowers in a playful dance.
Bees in pajamas buzz past,
While rabbits suggest a morning prance.

A rooster crowing, oh so proud,
Singing an off-key tune in the fog.
Crops wagging their leafy heads,
Planted jokes in the cololful bog.

Sunflowers turning their backs to the sun,
Whispering tales of the night's delight.
A cow on a mission, oh, what fun!
Chasing a butterfly, a quirky sight.

The trees laugh softly with a sway,
As seeds tumble down in a cheerful race.
Even the wind cracks a joke today,
Pushing clouds to giggle in their place.

A Canopy of Stars and Secrets

Underneath a twinkling spree,
Stars gather like friends having a blast.
Whispers of wishes tiptoe free,
While the moon plays cards, quite the cast.

Crickets chirp in a band unplanned,
Creating a symphony on the fly.
A raccoon in a mask, oh so grand,
Steals the show with a wink and sly.

Clouds roll in, like a cotton parade,
Making shapes that tease the keen eye.
An owl hoots, with a wise charade,
Nudging a squirrel who questions why.

Fireflies flicker, lighting the scene,
A dance floor for bugs, what a delight!
Nature's party—wild and serene,
A gathering that stretches through the night.

Laughter of Streams

The stream gurgles with a joyous howl,
Making rocks chuckle as they flow.
Fish flip flop, they can't help but prowl,
Dancing a jig, putting on a show.

Frogs leap in, giving raucous cheers,
Waving their legs like soft balloons.
Pebbles snicker, lost in their peers,
The water sings its merry tunes.

Willows sway with laughter so light,
Their branches tickle the fish below.
A splash of giggles, oh, what a sight,
As dragonflies glide, putting on a show.

Even the lilies join in the jest,
Wearing crowns made of dew and delight.
In the laughter, they find their rest,
Chasing the sun till it bids goodnight.

Silence of Stones

The stones sit still, plotting a prank,
Moss clings on, swaying in delight.
Each one has a secret to crank,
Whispering stories to the stars at night.

An old pebble chuckles, wise and spry,
Telling tales of mischievous waves.
While boulders ponder, asking why,
The ground giggles as the world behaves.

Squirrels tap-dance on a rock's face,
Chasing ants for a game of tag.
The silence bursts—their joyous race,
Nature's laughter in a leafy brag.

Underneath, the roots wiggle and spread,
Creating a floor for their comedic play.
Stones hold onto secrets unsaid,
As they bask in the sun's golden ray.

The Solace of Shadows and Glades

Shadows stretch like sleepy cats,
Chasing beams in a lazy chase.
Leaves rustle, wearing funny hats,
Embracing the breeze with a gentle grace.

In the glade, laughter echoes clear,
A deer prances with a skip so light.
A squirrel giggles, no sign of fear,
Challenging trees to a delightful fight.

Beneath the ferns, secrets unfold,
As critters plan their next big spree.
The outlines of laughter gently mold,
Creating a canvas for wild glee.

When twilight falls, the shadows blend,
Stars peep out from their cozy beds.
Nature whispers, with humor to lend,
Cracking jokes as day gracefully spreads.

Shadows Under the Ancient Oaks

In the shade of mighty trees,
Squirrels plot their grand charades.
Acorns fall like tiny bombs,
While birds laugh and serenade.

The roots twist like a joke well told,
Branches dance, they wiggle and sway.
A deer trips over her own feet,
Nature's comedy on display.

With laughter echoing all around,
Breezes carry giggles high.
Leafy hats and twiggy canes,
Who knew trees could make you cry?

Beneath the shade, we take our place,
Echoes of nature's playful tease.
Finding joy in every rustle,
As laughter floats on the breeze.

Harmony Found in Feathered Song

Chirping birds with silly calls,
They chatter like they're at a show.
A parrot thinks he's quite a star,
Preening feathers, putting on a glow.

The robin falls into a squawk,
As blue jays steal the shady spot.
With every warble, there's a laugh,
It's a feathery improv plot.

Seagulls squabble, yelling 'Mine!'
While woodpeckers think they're grand.
The concert's full of silly tunes,
Nature's band, an unplanned band.

As frogs join in with croaks and ribbits,
They harmonize, a comedic jam.
Nature's stage, no need for scripts,
Just laughter, feathers, and plenty of glam.

The Soft Touch of Twilight

Twilight whispers in a soft tone,
As fireflies twinkle like stars.
A raccoon snickers at the dark,
While crickets strum their guitar bars.

The sun yawns, stretching wide awake,
As shadows play their peekaboo.
The moon chuckles, shining bright,
While owls hoot in a slight curfew.

In the soft glow, laughter swells,
With beetles marching like a parade.
A hedgehog rolls, a fuzzy ball,
In the twilight, joy is made.

As night unfolds its furry arms,
Critters dance, a happy spree.
In this gentle, funny twilight,
Nature chuckles, wild and free.

Embraced by Mossy Delights

Moss covers rocks like a fluffy coat,
Turtles wear it like fine attire.
The mushrooms peek, they wave hello,
While frogs croak jokes that never tire.

A worm wiggles, doing a dance,
The snails glide slowly with great flair.
Each plop of raindrop leads to giggles,
As the moss grows without a care.

Friends gather, the critters unite,
For a feast on leaves with roots to share.
Laughter bubbles up in the moist air,
Among the nature's grand buffet affair.

Here in the bliss of earthy charm,
Everything's cozy, snug, and bright.
With moss as pillows and stones as seats,
In this playground, everything feels right.

Nature's Caress, a Gentle Lullaby

The trees hum songs, oh what a show,
While squirrels gossip in a row.
The flowers giggle, swaying in glee,
A butterfly winks, just at me.

The brook is chuckling, can't you hear?
It spills the secrets, oh dear, oh dear!
A frog leaps by with a silly croak,
Is nature laughing? Oh, what a joke!

Beneath the sun, the daisies dance,
Each little bee takes a happy chance.
With every breeze, there's a playful tease,
Nature's humor put me at ease.

The clouds parade, shapes twist and bend,
A pizza slice? Or maybe a friend?
In this garden of giggles and cheer,
I found my joy, it's perfectly clear.

Dreams Woven in Whispering Grasses

The grasses sway, a ticklish scene,
Whispers float by, sharp and keen.
Each blade confides a secret or two,
Like, 'Did you see what the turtle could do?'

Fireflies blink like tiny stars,
They flash their lights, playing guitars.
Crickets chirp with comedic flair,
Singing tunes, without a care.

A rabbit hops, his ears are long,
He trips on roots, where he belongs.
With every bounce, I'm sure he'd say,
'Nature's a clown, come join the play!'

As shadows stretch in the waning light,
Laughter rolls on into the night.
In this wild stage, my heart will stay,
Where dreams and giggles lead the way.

Unraveling Time Under the Stars

Stars twinkle bright like diamonds tossed,
Under their gaze, we never feel lost.
The moon winks down, a sly little spy,
Dropping silly jokes from way up high.

The owls hoot with a wise old flair,
While raccoons plot and the night grows rare.
"Who let the chickens play outside?" they ask,
As shadows dance—a night-time task.

Time ticks slowly when the crickets sing,
Each note a promise, and joy they bring.
Just one firefly? No, hold your applause!
A thousand more join, oh what a cause!

In this gathering, I shed my fright,
As laughter bursts like stars in the night.
With nature's charm, I feel so free,
What a crazy world, just here with me!

Echoing Heartbeats in the Forest

Amidst the trees, a heartbeats' race,
Woodpeckers drum their lively bass.
Bouncing logs and laughing leaves,
Nature giggles, everyone believes.

A falling branch gives a silly scare,
But watch it crash! A comical affair!
The bushes rustle with joyous snaps,
Squirrels hold court with acorn mishaps.

Each step I take invites a chuckle,
"Did you see that?" nature whispers, in a shuffle.
With every rustle, a humorous tune,
This forest hosts a wild cartoon.

As stars come out, the mischief takes flight,
The moon beams down, what a goofy sight!
From every corner, laughter ripples wide,
In this funny nook, I'll always abide.

The Gentle Call of the Stream

The water burbles, slightly rude,
A fish pokes out, who's in the mood.
It splashes back, the splash was grand,
And nods at ducks, to lend a hand.

The rocks all giggle, round and smooth,
As little frogs jump, trying to groove.
Mosquitoes zoom, like tiny spies,
They whisper secrets, oh how time flies!

A squirrel shimmies, thinking he's sly,
Stealing snacks, thinking no one's nigh.
The sun winks down, a warm embrace,
While dragonflies dance, in silly grace.

So here we sit, beside the flow,
With giggles shared, and tales to show.
In every ripple, life's a scene,
Where laughter reigns, as frogs convene.

Echoes of the Earth's Breath

The mountains chuckle, standing tall,
With rocks that wobble, and squirrels that sprawl.
The soil whispers, with a gentle tease,
As ants march on, like little fees.

Clouds drift by, in cotton candy,
While rainbows pop, oh isn't it dandy?
A wind chime clinks, oh what a sound,
As perfumed breezes joyously abound.

The trees converse with rustling leaves,
They gossip freely, like mischievous thieves.
A squirrel overhears, then starts to plot,
To play a trick, oh what a thought!

So nature giggles, in shades and hues,
Painting moments in laughter-infused views.
With every breath, it shows its smile,
In echoes loud, let's linger awhile.

Solitude Amongst the Pines

The pines are pretty, oh so serene,
But wait! A squirrel's become a queen.
She rules the branches with quite a flair,
Dropping acorns like jewels for a fair.

The shadows lurk, play hide and seek,
With whispers buzzing, they spend the week.
The groundhog pops, his head on a stick,
He rolls his eyes, my, what a trick!

A raccoon jokes, with mischief at hand,
Stealing snacks just as he planned.
The trees seem puzzled, they softly sway,
What's next on the agenda for this playful day?

Amidst the pines, where time will bend,
Laughter echoes, like a dear friend.
In every creak, a tale is spun,
In solitude's arms, we find the fun!

When Leaves Dance with the Wind

The leaves all shimmy, stating their case,
Crisp and crunchy, in wild embrace.
They tell each other, secrets and dreams,
As the wind chuckles, or so it seems.

A rabbit hops, with toes that tap,
Joining the leaves in a merry clap.
They spin and twirl, in a dizzy spree,
While nearby ants plan a great jubilee.

Clouds drift lazily, with faces so round,
As the sun giggles at the joy it found.
With every rustle, a chorus sings,
Creating stories on gentle wings.

So as the twilight brings day to an end,
The leaves whisper tales, around the bend.
With laughter to share, in this playful land,
Where joy dances softly, hand in hand.

Starlight on Sleepy Valleys

Stars twinkle like fireflies caught in a jar,
The hills snicker softly, 'What a strange bazaar!'
The owls host a party, but hush! No loud cheer,
For rabbits wear top hats, sipping their beer.

Moonbeams dance playfully on patches of grass,
While crickets crack jokes, they're lovely first class.
The shadows are laughing, they wiggle with glee,
"Who stole my sandwich?" asks a wobbly tree!

Squirrels juggle acorns, a daring charade,
The raccoons go wild, "Is this masquerade?"
Fireflies light up with their blink and their flash,
A turtle remarks, "Oh, what a smash!"

Giggles echo softly through night's gentle veil,
While sleepy-eyed badgers start plotting a trail.
The valleys all slumber as stars shine so bright,
In their world of laughter, they giggle at night.

Nature's Secret Sanctuary

In the grove where the tall trees wear wigged-out hats,
A snail tells a tale—"Oh, where are the mats?"
The ladybugs gossip, as butterflies spin,
About how grasshoppers always jump in.

Petunias discuss their newest hairdo,
While daisies strut proudly in the morning dew.
The rocks play along, pretending to sleep,
Yet they crack up each time the bunnies leap.

Clouds drift by joking about hair-dos so plush,
While the river flows on with a cheerful hush.
The fish in the brook chuckle, making a splash,
As frogs croak their secrets, all wrapped in a bash!

Every twig whispers with wisdom and grace,
As gusts of wind tease, "Come join our race!"
In this natural laughter, all worries take flight,
Where every leaf laughs in the warmth of the night.

A Stroll Through Whispering Leaves

With every step taken, the leaves share a joke,
As squirrels roll their eyes, "Oh, what a bloke!"
A broomstick's a stand-up, all branches applaud,
While the grass claims the role of a slippery fraud.

Cartwheeling flowers in technicolor bloom,
Invite accompanying bees to their zoom.
But watch out for spiders, they prank from above,
Their webs spin surprises like handwoven love!

A turtle on the path shouts, "I'm quick! I swear!"
While snickering frogs croak, "Just look at that hair!"
The wind's an old jokester, it tickles the trees,
With laughter so hearty, it brings you to your knees.

While crickets compose a symphony of cheer,
A mouse hits the high notes that everyone hears.
In this stroll through whispers, the world feels so bright,
Nature's humor unfolds in the soft, shimm'ring light.

Between the Boughs of Memory

Between the boughs where the shadows conspire,
The ants throw a party by the old gate wire.
They dance on the stones, clapping tiny hands,
While the sun winks over the raucous bands.

The trees tell tall tales of a squirrel so bold,
Who stole half the acorns from neighbors of old.
The bees roll their eyes, buzzing chaotically,
"Why can't they just share?" It's truly a mockery!

A porcupine prances, he's dressed in a suit,
With spines like a quill, he refuses to boot.
The beetles debate about fashion and flair,
As each one accessorizes with style and care.

The sunlight spins laughter, weaving through leaves,
As flowers exchange gossip, oh how it weaves!
In this woods of memories, lighthearted and bright,
Every bough is an echo of joy and pure delight.

A Symphony of Stillness

The trees are swaying, giving a cheer,
A squirrel's debate on who's the best deer.
The birds hold a concert, they miss a few notes,
A tune that's for squirrels, not one for the goats.

The sun wears a hat, so stylish and neat,
While rabbits gossip, a gossiping feat.
A snail races by, oh what a slow show,
He'll reach the finish, just very, very slow.

The crickets are chirping their finest grand song,
While frogs do the disco, they'll dance all night long.
The breeze brings the giggles of leaves up above,
Nature is funny, and full of good love.

So grab your delight and join in the fun,
When nature plays jokes, it's a laugh for everyone.
Just remember to smile at the wonders you see,
For life in the wild can be quite zany!

Tranquil Moments by the Lake

The ducks in a row, all quack in a line,
While fish leap in joy, it's a splashy divine.
The turtles sunbathe, so cool and composed,
While bugs play their music, so oddly juxtaposed.

A frog in a tux, what a sight to behold,
Hopping to music, quite graceful and bold.
He slips on a lily, but lands with a grin,
"Did you see that? My dance won't begin!"

The breeze brings warm laughter from trees all around,
While beavers build homes, they make quite a sound.
They're crafting their cabins, a fine little mess,
Nature's DIY, what a crafty success!

At dusk, fireflies flash, like tiny disco balls,
As stars join the fun with their shimmering calls.
Together they twinkle, in a dance so unique,
Laughing at night in the calm by the creek.

Secrets of the Verdant Hollow

Deep in the hollow, where the whispers are loose,
Worms in tuxedos discuss the best juice.
The oak tickles elf feet, who giggle and play,
As mushrooms hold parties at night, come what may.

The hedgehog's a poet, his rhymes are a treat,
While the fox plays guitar, oh, what a sweet beat!
The toads start a band—that sounds quite bizarre,
Their concert's a hit with the critters so far.

The flowers exchange tales of colors and scents,
"Who wore it best?" is the floral pretense.
As dew drops are jewels in the morning sun's light,
Nature's gathering laughter, a wonderful sight!

If trees could share secrets, they'd spill all they found,
About pranks played by critters, so merry and sound.
In this hollow of mischief, all life's quite a show,
With giggles and chuckles, what joy in the flow!

Caress of the Morning Dew

Morning arrives with a swoosh and a cheer,
Dew drops like diamonds, they're shimmering here.
A grasshopper hops, with a spring quite amusing,
As the sun starts to laugh, the shadows are losing.

The daisies all giggle, with heads high in glee,
While butterflies wonder, "Is that honey for me?"
The ants march in rhythm, a brigade with a cause,
To bring back the crumbs, earning nature's applause.

A cheeky raccoon steals a berry or two,
With a grin on his face, who knew he could chew?
The morning unfolds with a whimsical tune,
As each leaf sways gently, all in good fortune.

So let's welcome the morning, with laughter and light,
For nature's a jester, in sun's golden sight.
In this joyful embrace, every creature will muse,
Together they dance in the caress of the dews.

Whispers of the Wandering Breeze

A squirrel holds a nut so tight,
While birds in hats take their flight.
The trees gossip as leaves do sway,
And mushrooms giggle at the play.

A rabbit hops with flair and grace,
While bugs have their little race.
The sun's a jester, bright and bold,
Telling tales of warmth untold.

Caterpillars strut like they own the scene,
While ants march on, all dressed in green.
The breeze, it snickers, light and fast,
At nature's party, we're all outclassed.

And as the day begins to fade,
The moon points out the stars displayed.
In this silliness, we find our cheer,
Nature's laughter - music to the ear!

Solitude Beneath Canopy Skies

Under leaves, the shadows play,
A snail rehearses its slow ballet.
A raccoon once tried on my shoe,
Said it fit him, how about you?

The owls hoot in quirky tones,
While frogs party on moist stones.
Bees serenade the blooms in pink,
And hold a dance-off near the creek.

In solitude, but never lonely,
The nature club feels so homely.
With laughter echoes that never cease,
Our woodland lives brought forth in peace.

Each rustle, hum, each vibrant tune,
Plays harmonies beneath the moon.
With silly antics all around,
In nature's arms, pure joy is found.

The Harmony of Silent Woods

Amidst the trunks, a fox does freeze,
Trying to blend in with the trees.
But with that tail, it's hard to hide,
Nature chuckles, filled with pride.

The shadows dance with every sway,
And mushrooms throw their own soiree.
Crickets chirp in awkward tunes,
While raccoons moonwalk under moons.

The wind tells secrets, oh so sly,
As birds play tag up in the sky.
With every rustling, there's a shout,
A giggle from the critters about.

The woods may seem like calm and still,
But listen close, there's crazy thrill!
For every hush, there's laughter near,
Nature's joy, loud and clear.

Echoes of Earth's Gentle Breath

The groundhog peeks from beneath the ground,
In shades of brown, he prances 'round.
He rolls and tumbles, all in fun,
While clouds above play hide and run.

A clam digs deep to hide its face,
While puddles leap with frog-like grace.
With beetles donning tiny shades,
The sun turns up and truly cascades.

In whispers soft, the crickets tease,
While bumblebees dance with gentle ease.
As summer's pulse begins to hum,
The trees applauded, 'Here they come!'

Nature chuckles with every breeze,
In this big world, whatever please.
So join the laughter, don't hold back,
For life's a joke, on this green track!

The Color of Silence

When the trees gossip, they rustle so loud,
And squirrels debate who's wearing the crown.
The flower's pink blushing, a rambling clown,
While shadows just giggle beneath a soft shroud.

Birds chirrup with rhythm, but still lose their beat,
As leaves swirl around like they're dancing a jig.
In a world where the sun just can't quite find its seat,
The wind tells a joke with a swish and a swig.

Rocky paths chuckle, their pebbles in tow,
Mice make a sneak peek, but nothing to say.
The daisies are laughing; they put on a show,
In the stillness of green, they just frolic and play.

So join this parade of the odd and the sweet,
Where whispers of laughter float through the air.
The color of silence has never felt neat,
But humor's the thread that weaves joy everywhere.

Ferns and Fragments of a Dream

In a forest of ferns where the oddities bloom,
Lizards wear ties, held with vines and with pride.
Mushrooms are giggling, and giving a loom,
While trees share secrets that they've tried to hide.

A frog on a lily is playing a tune,
His croak's like a hoot, as he strums at the night.
Fireflies join in, flickering in June,
Weaving a melody, dimming the light.

Naps under a toadstool bring dreams of dessert,
While bees lip-sync pop songs, can't seem to keep time.
Each whimsy sets laughter in motion, not hurt,
And the breeze keeps it rolling, like lyrics in rhyme.

So take off those shoes, let your toes wiggle free,
In this odd little realm, where no worries are found.
With each fern and fragment, just be what you see,
And let all the giggles spin round like a sound.

Still Waters Flowing Deep

Reflections glimmer like a barbecue grill,
Fish fashion their fins in synchronized style.
A duck with a quack that could flatten a hill,
Counts ripples like sheep, with a confident smile.

The moon floats above, wearing a face full of cheese,
While frogs create symphonies, joyous and spry.
A boat with no rowers paddles as it please,
Just drifting along, laughing as it goes by.

Stone by the bank thinks it's quite the hot shot,
Debating with snails on who's slower at life.
In water's embrace, all darting about,
Each splash a comic twist, hilarious strife.

So let the quiet giggles of nature abound,
In still waters flowing, we've found such delight.
With humor and wonder, life twirls around,
It's the joy of the depths that keeps hearts feeling light.

The Abode of Lost Conversations

Where whispers get tangled, a breeze starts to sass,
Gossiping leaves have quite tales to unfold.
The rocks roll their eyes, fed up with their past,
As chips of old bark share their stories, half-told.

A stream's chattering bubbles, like laughter in bars,
Share secrets of fish who are awkwardly shy.
Clouds plot and plan, with the sky full of stars,
While shadows eavesdrop, saying 'Oh my, oh my!'

The nook of lost phrases has critters who scheme,
Each hedgehog prepares for a stand-up routine.
A snail picks the punchlines, slicker than cream,
While the world around chuckles, all feeling serene.

So let's join the laughter, this uproarious place,
Where whispers and jokes ruffle through every leaf.
In this abode of chatter, it's laughter we chase,
And joy we discover, like nature's chief belief.

Petals Fall Like Time

Petals flutter down like they forgot their cue,
They tumble about, in a swirling dance, it's true.
An audience of ants, wagging tiny heads,
Say, "Look at that bloom, it's dancing, not dead!"

Bees buzz by, wearing their frowning attire,
Wondering if petals have started a choir.
"Is it time for tea, or a picnic to share?"
Each flower seems to grin, without a moment to spare!

Sun shines down, playing tricks on the bee,
"Caught in a whirlwind of pollen debris!"
While squirrels conspire, planning their next feat,
A heist for the snacks that they think are a treat.

So let petals reveal their humor sublime,
Falling like laughter, as if stealing time.
They chuckle and giggle, a whimsical bunch,
Who'd thought that blooms could throw such a punch?

The Calm Between Raindrops

Raindrops dance like they're wearing tap shoes,
Each one a performer with rosy red hues.
A puddle looks up, winks at a cloud,
"If I were a dancer, could I draw a crowd?"

The sky grumbles softly, a wise guy's remark,
"You won't steal my spotlight; I've got room in the dark!"
Each droplet quips back, as they plop on the ground,
"We've got our routines, and our talent knows no bound!"

Leaves shimmy and shake, just trying to stay dry,
While worms poke their heads, giving it a try.
"I'm not swimming today," says the old wrinkled oak,
Amused by the mischief, laughing like it's a joke.

So let pitter-patter bring giggles, not dread,
For even the storm clouds wear smiles overhead.
In the splash of the puddles, a chuckle ensues,
As nature holds court, in her silver-lined hues.

Embracing the Solitude of Skies

Clouds float by, with a flair for the fun,
Dressing up like cotton candy on the run.
"Hey sun, quit hogging the limelight, my friend!"
Like they float with a joke that they never quite end.

Birds chirp in tune, rehearsing all day,
Singing ballads of breadcrumbs and haphazard play.
They argue and squabble, it's all very nice,
About who gets first dibs on the piece of rice!

A kite in the distance, with a grin on its face,
Says, "Why fly straight? I'll just dance in this space!"
While wind whispers secrets, tickles trees just right,
It's a performance of nature that's pure delight.

So look up and laugh; let worries take flight,
In a sky full of joy, there's no need for fright.
A world of blithe chuckles, adorned with a sky,
Where whimsy takes wing, and the giggles soar high!

Serenity in the Flicker of Fireflies

Fireflies twinkle, like stars in a jar,
Casting their glow, from near and from far.
"Hey, I'm outshining you!" one flickers with glee,
While another zips by, saying, "Look at me!"

They flit and they dance, in a waltz of delight,
With an impish charm that turns dark into light.
"No need for the moon, we're a party of sparks!"
They chuckle and play, illuminating parks.

Crickets join in, with their offbeat tune,
As they pull on their shoes, all set for a boon.
"Let's form a band!" chirps the bold lead singer,
While the other bugs hum, and join in a zinger.

So savor the evening, where laughter takes flight,
In a world of soft twinkles, where wishes grow bright.
The language of laughter, in the night's warm embrace,
Is the secret of joy that all nature can trace!

The Heartbeat of the Forest Floor

Amidst the leaves, so crisp and bright,
A squirrel plots its daring flight.
It leaps on high, then slips away,
I giggle loud—the tree's ballet!

The ants are marching in a line,
With tiny helmets, oh so fine!
They gather crumbs, their grand parade,
While I'm just here, with lemonade.

A raccoon sneaks without a care,
His mask on tight, he's quite the air.
But one loud crunch, he drops his loot,
I laugh so hard, he takes a scoot!

The forest shakes with laughter, too,
As birds join in, a funny crew.
They chirp and squawk, a joyous sound,
Where clumsy critters all are found.

Shadows Play in Woodland Glow

The light breaks through, a playful dance,
Shadows skip in a whimsical trance.
A twig snaps loud, the mushrooms clap,
I chuckle soft, it's nature's rap!

The owls hoot jokes in midnight's breath,
While crickets chirp the tales of death.
But who would think that laughter's near,
While bogs and brambles hide their cheer?

A fox in shades, so sly and spry,
Winks at me with a knowing eye.
He slips on leaves, who'd have foreseen?
The forest floor—a comic scene!

Mossy stones, they giggle too,
As I tumble down, with quite a view.
Nature's jesters, wild and free,
In every nook, a comedy!

The Allure of Untamed Wilderness

Upon the trail, I try to tread,
When suddenly, a branch gets wedged.
I do a dance, a clumsy twist,
Nature laughs, I can't resist!

Bushes whisper secrets low,
While butterflies put on a show.
I chase them lightly, what a sight,
But lose my shoe—it just took flight!

A beaver builds with much delight,
He adds a twig, then shuffles right.
His little log—my biggest foe,
He grins at me, "Oh, you know so!"

The breeze carries giggles, it seems,
As I trip over hidden dreams.
With every scratch and muddy grin,
The wild weaves laughter deep within.

A Breath Taken in Stillness

Amid the trees, I pause to breathe,
A bumblebee takes off, and heaves.
He buzzes loud, a tiny jet,
I duck and laugh, it's quite a bet!

The squirrels gossip in the shade,
I swear they jest, in furry trade.
They plot the day, with acorn forks,
While I sip tea, and laugh at quirks.

The breeze ruffles my floppy hat,
A deer pops up, a silent brat.
With one quick glance, it springs away,
Next time, I'll wear some disco sway!

The world around hums with delight,
From nature's care, I feel so right.
With chuckles here and giggles there,
I find my peace, in sunny air.

www.ingramcontent.com/pod-product-compliance
Ingram Content Group UK Ltd.
Pitfield, Milton Keynes, MK11 3LW, UK
UKHW022106050225
454743UK00006B/104

9 783690 812245